Starting Cooking

Gill Harvey

Designed by Sarah Bealham
and Maria Wheatley
Illustrated by Norman Young
Photography by Amanda Heywood
Edited by Fiona Watt

Cookery specialist: Julia Kirby-Jones
Food stylist: Carole Handslip
Cover and additional photography
by Howard Allman

Contents

Before you begin

For a link to a website where you can read tips on how to keep a kitchen clean and how to avoid accidents, go to www.usborne-quicklinks.com

This book shows you how to start cooking using rings or burners, a grill and an oven. It explains many of the skills that will help you to cook and gives lots of tasty recipes for you to try.

A recipe tells you how to make something to eat. It has a list of the food you will need, called the ingredients. It also tells you which things to use. These are called kitchen utensils. Here you can see most of the utensils you will use in this book.

Staying clean

Roll up your sleeves. Wash your hands and put on an apron.

Always use clean utensils and wash everything up afterwards.

Wipe surfaces clean with a damp cloth. Wipe up anything that you spill on the floor straight away.

 Vegetarian food

Vegetarians are people who don't eat meat or fish. Recipes with this picture next to them can be eaten by vegetarians.

Rolling pin

Grater

Mixing bowl

Sieve

Saucepan

Colander

Lemon squeezer

Chopping board

Pudding basin

Keeping safe

Before you start, make sure there is an adult nearby to help you. Never leave the kitchen when rings or burners or the grill are on, and don't try to carry hot things that are too heavy for you.

Fish slice

Rounded knife

Kitchen knives

Tin opener

Ask an adult for help when you see this picture. Always ask for help when you turn on an electric cooker, or if you need to light a gas cooker.

Take extra care when you see this picture. For example, be very careful when using sharp knives. Turn saucepan handles so they don't stick out.

This picture warns you that something is very hot. When you touch anything hot, wear oven gloves to protect you. Put hot things onto a heat-proof mat.

Remember to turn off rings or burners, the grill or the oven when you have finished with them. This picture reminds you when to turn something off.

Getting ready

Before you start cooking, read the recipe right through. Each one is enough for four people unless it says something else. Check that you have all the ingredients and utensils.

When you see a cooking skill written in **bold**, look at the bottom of the page. There you can find out where it is first explained. You can also find out more about cooking skills if you look on page 32.

Cake tins

Whisk

Oven glove

Pastry brush

Vegetable peeler

Spatula

Wooden spoon

Baking tray

3

Getting started

When you cook, you weigh things like flour and sugar with scales. Add them to the scales bit by bit. Stop when you reach the right weight.

This book gives two ways to measure your ingredients, by metric measures or by imperial measures. Follow one list or the other.

Metric measurements	Imperial measurements
grams(g)	ounces(oz)
millilitres(ml)	pounds(lbs)
litres(l)	pints

A pinch is a very small amount of something like salt or pepper. It is what you can pick up between your finger and thumb.

You use a measuring jug to measure liquids like milk and fruit juice. Pour them in slowly until they reach the right mark on the jug.

Put the jug onto a flat surface.

Tablespoons and teaspoons are used to measure small amounts. Tablespoon is written "tbs" and teaspoon is written "tsp".

A level spoon

A rounded spoon

A heaped spoon

Crunchy muesli

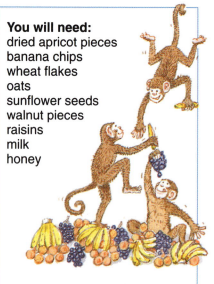

You will need:
dried apricot pieces
banana chips
wheat flakes
oats
sunflower seeds
walnut pieces
raisins
milk
honey

scales, big bowl, tablespoon, measuring jug, teaspoon

You could put fresh fruit into the muesli, such as peaches or strawberries. Add them just before you eat it.

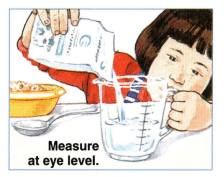

Measure
at eye level.

Weigh 50g (2oz) oats and put them into a big bowl. Add 50g (2oz) wheat flakes, 50g (2oz) banana chips and 50g (2oz) apricot pieces.

Add 2 rounded tbs raisins, 1 rounded tbs sunflower seeds and 3 rounded tbs walnuts. Mix everything together well.

Put into four dishes. Measure 150ml (¼ pint) of milk for each dish. Pour it over. Add 1 tsp of honey to each dish if you like sweet muesli.

Parts of a cooker

The two main types of cooker are electric and gas. They usually have four rings or burners, a grill and an oven.

A grill and its control knob may be above or below the rings or burners. If your grill is hard to reach, ask an adult to help you.

Here you can see some types of oven knob. Fan ovens are different, so if you have one you need to read your instruction book.

Control knobs

Grill

Oven

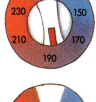

Gas oven

This oven is set at Gas Mark 2. This is a low heat for cooking things slowly.

Each ring or burner has its own knob to control the heat. You can make each one hotter or cooler by turning the knob.

Recipes in this book give temperatures in °C, °F and gas. They also tell you which shelf you should cook your food on.

Electric oven (°C)

This oven is set at medium heat. This can be between 160°C and 190°C.

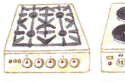

Gas burners

Electric rings

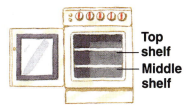

Top shelf

Middle shelf

Electric oven (°F)

This oven is set at 450°F. This is a hot oven, for cooking things like bread.

5

Using a grill

A grill cooks things very quickly on one side. To cook them on the other side, you have to turn them over. This can be tricky because the grill pan and the food you are grilling become very hot, so ask an adult to help.

Cheese and ham toasties

For one toastie you will need:
2 slices white or brown bread
butter or margarine
1 slice cooked ham
50g (2oz) cheese
a tomato
some cucumber

grater
small plate
rounded knife
oven gloves
tongs
kitchen knife
chopping board

You can make vegetarian toasties by leaving out the ham. You could add tomato instead.

To make a cheese and tomato toastie, put some slices of tomato on top of the grated cheese before grilling it.

Grating

Put the grater on a plate. Hold it tightly with the holes you want to use facing away from you.

Hold the piece of food firmly and push it down the holes on the grater. Do this lots of times.

Stop grating when your fingers get close to the grater. A small piece of food will be left over.

Use a rounded knife.

Grate the cheese onto a plate. Turn the grill to full heat. Spread butter on the slices of bread.

Lay the second slice of bread on top of the ham and cheese. The butter should be on the outside.

Use tongs

Pull the grill pan out. Turn the toastie over carefully, then grill it on the other side until it goes brown.

Turn one slice over so the butter is underneath. Put the slice of ham onto it. Sprinkle the cheese on top.

Place the toastie on the grill rack and slide the pan under the grill. Watch it carefully until it goes brown.

Cut the toastie into triangles. Cut slices of cucumber and tomato. Arrange them on a plate around the toastie.

Chopping and slicing

To chop a tomato, hold it firmly, making a bridge with your fingers. Cut it in half. Put the halves down flat. Chop them in half again. Keep chopping until the pieces are the size you want them.

To slice a tomato, cut down one side. Keep your fingers well away from the knife.

Try to cut thin slices.

To slice a cucumber, hold it firmly at one end. Cut thin slices from the other end.

Using an oven

Most ovens need time to heat up, so you need to turn them on before you start cooking. To do this, turn the oven knob to the temperature given in the recipe. Usually,  this makes a light come on which goes out when the oven is hot enough. Remember that if you have a fan oven it may be different, so check in your instruction book.

Baked potatoes

For two potatoes you will need:
2 large baking potatoes
cooking oil
butter or margarine

For the fillings, choose:
200g (7oz) tin tuna
1 tbs mayonnaise
200g (7oz) tin sweetcorn
or:
75g (3oz) cheese
pickle

stiff brush for cleaning potatoes, fork, kitchen paper, baking tray, oven gloves, kitchen knife, tin opener, tablespoon, small bowl, grater, plate, teaspoon

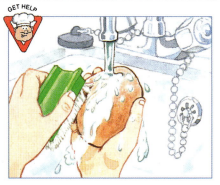

Turn the oven on to 200°C (400°F, Gas Mark 6). Scrub the potatoes with the brush in cold water.

Put the tray of potatoes into the oven. Cook them for about one hour, then take them out carefully.

If they are still hard, cook them for another 30 minutes and test them again. If they are soft, cut them in half.

Prick the potatoes all over with a fork. Wipe on some oil with kitchen paper. Put them onto a baking tray.

Test the potatoes with a kitchen knife. If they are cooked, they will feel soft all the way through.

Put a little butter or margarine into each potato. Put the filling you have chosen on top (see right).

For a link to a website where you can play a fast-moving game called Potato Snake, go to www.usborne-quicklinks.com

Using a microwave

GET HELP

Microwaves cook food more quickly than other ovens.

Never put anything metal in a microwave.

To cook potatoes, prick them with a fork. Put them into the microwave on kitchen paper. You will need to look in your instruction book to find out how long to cook them for.

Try a filling of soured cream and chopped chives.

Tuna, mayonnaise and sweetcorn filling

GET HELP

Pile the filling onto the potato.

Open the tins of tuna and sweetcorn. You may need an adult to help.

Drain the liquid from the tins by holding down the lid and tipping it into the sink.

Put the tuna into a small bowl. Mix in the mayonnaise and 2 tbs sweetcorn.

Tuna, mayonnaise and sweetcorn filling, and cheese filling.

Cheese and pickle filling

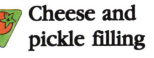

Grate the cheese onto a plate. Put half on each potato. Add some pickle with a teaspoon.

9

Baking cakes

When you bake a cake, you may be tempted to open the oven door half-way through cooking to check it. This can make the cake sink in the middle, so wait until it is almost cooked before you have a look.

Brownies

You will need:

100g (4oz) margarine
250g (8oz) soft brown sugar
2 eggs
50g (2oz) chopped walnuts
100g (4oz) self-raising flour
40g (1½oz) cocoa
1 level tsp baking powder

small square or oblong tin (about 23 x 23 cm/9 x 9in), scissors, greaseproof paper, kitchen paper, wooden spoon, mixing bowl, small bowl, fork, sieve, metal spoon, oven gloves, kitchen knife, wire rack

Mixing bowl

Turn the oven to 180°C (350°F, Gas Mark 4). Grease and line the tin. Cream the margarine and sugar.

Crack the eggs by tapping them sharply on the edge of a bowl. Carefully break them in half into the bowl.

Greasing and lining tins

To grease a tin, dip some kitchen paper in margarine. Wipe it all over the inside of the tin. Make sure you reach right to the edge.

To line a tin, draw around it on greaseproof paper. Draw another square around it, big enough to cover the sides of the tin.

Cut out the big square. Cut from the edge to the four corners of the small square. Fold up the edges. Fit the paper into the tin.

For a link to a website where you can learn how to make "Batty Buns" for Hallowe'en (or anytime!), go to www.usborne-quicklinks.com

Mix the yolks and whites with a fork. Add slowly to the sugar and margarine, beating all the time.

Mix in the walnuts. Spoon the flour, cocoa and baking powder into a sieve. Shake into the mixture. Fold in.

Use the middle shelf.

Cook for five more minutes if not cooked.

Spoon the mixture into the tin. Smooth the top with the spoon. Cook for 40 minutes, then take it out.

Press the top of the cake lightly. It will spring back into shape when you lift your finger if it is cooked.

You could sprinkle icing sugar over the squares.

Allow to cool for ten minutes, then cut the cake into squares with a kitchen knife. Put onto a wire rack.

Beating, folding and creaming

Beating means mixing firmly with a wooden spoon or an electric mixer. Ask an adult to help with a mixer.

Creaming is beating margarine or butter and sugar together so that they become a smooth mixture.

To fold in, you mix gently with a metal spoon or flat knife. Try to burst as few bubbles of air as possible.

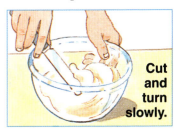

Cut and turn slowly.

11

Meaty oven dishes

When you cook meat in an oven you can add lots of things to it like herbs and vegetables, which make it really tasty. This is because the meat takes quite a long time to cook, so the different flavours have plenty of time to get into it. The taste of the meat makes the vegetables delicious, too.

You can find out how to cook rice to eat with your chicken on pages 20-21.

Cooking chicken

Always wash chicken before you cook it. If it is frozen, make sure it is thawed right through. Always wash your hands after touching raw chicken, and check that it is properly cooked before you eat it.

Chicken parcels

You will need:
4 chicken quarters
100g (4oz) mushrooms
1 small red pepper
1 small green pepper
1 small onion
50g (2oz) margarine
  or butter
1 lemon
salt

kitchen paper, kitchen knife, chopping board, kitchen foil, scissors, lemon squeezer, baking tray, oven gloves

GET HELP

Turn the oven to 200°C (400°F, Gas Mark 6). Wash the chicken under the cold tap. Pat it dry with kitchen paper.

TAKE CARE

Wash and chop the mushrooms. Wash the peppers and slice them up. Peel the onion and chop it into thin strips.

12

Cut four squares of foil, each big enough to wrap around a piece of chicken. Put a piece in the middle of each one.

Share the vegetables between the pieces, then wash your hands. Dab on some margarine or butter. Add a pinch of salt.

Push down and twist.

Cut the lemon in half with a kitchen knife. Squeeze the juice from one half and sprinkle it over the chicken.

Fold the foil around the pieces, folding over twice on top, then twice at each end. Put the parcels on a baking tray.

Use the top shelf

Cook for one hour. Take the tray out and open the foil, being careful of the steam. Cook uncovered for 10-15 minutes.

Test by sticking a kitchen knife into the meat. If it is cooked, the meat will be white right through to the bone.

More chopping and slicing

To chop an onion, hold it firmly. Cut off both ends, then peel off all the brown skin.

Put the onion on one end. Hold it making a bridge with your fingers. Chop it in half.

Put the flat sides down and cut across in strips. You can then cut each strip into little pieces.

To chop a pepper, hold it at the thinner end and slice off the end with the stalk.

Take out the rest of the stalk and the core. Scrape the seeds from inside the pepper.

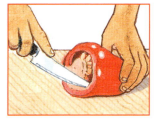

Slice the pepper into rounds or strips. You can then chop them into smaller pieces if you want.

Using rings or burners

For a link to a website where you can ask a chef a question about cooking, go to **www.usborne-quicklinks.com**

Rings and burners can give a very high heat. This means you need to watch carefully as you cook to make sure the food doesn't boil over the edge of the pan. You can stop things from sticking to the bottom of the pan by stirring with a wooden spoon.

Boiling and simmering

To bring something to the boil, turn the ring or burner to full heat. When the food bubbles a lot, it is boiling.

To simmer something bring it to the boil, then turn the heat down until the food is bubbling just a little bit.

Summer pudding

You will need:
750g (1½lb) fresh or frozen soft fruit (raspberries, black or redcurrants, blackberries, strawberries or bilberries)
125g (5oz) sugar
2 tbs water
10-12 slices white bread

colander, medium saucepan, wooden spoon, chopping board, kitchen knife, pudding basin, cup, small plate, weight such as tins, large plate

Put all the fruit into a colander. Wash it under a tap. Pull off all the leaves and stalks with your fingers.

Put the fruit, water and sugar into a saucepan. Place on a ring or burner and bring to the boil.

Try not to break up the fruit.

Turn down the heat and simmer the mixture for five minutes. Stir very gently with a wooden spoon.

Make the slices overlap.

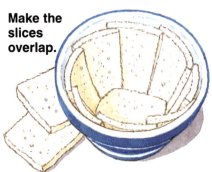

Cut the crusts off the slices of bread. Line the basin with the slices. Save two or three of them for the top.

Spoon the fruit into the basin. Save half a cup of fruit for later. Put the rest of the bread on top.

You could try summer pudding with cream.

Winter pudding

Winter pudding is made in exactly the same way as summer pudding, but with different fruit.

You will need:
500g (1lb) satsumas
100g (4oz) dried apple
100g (4oz) dried apricot
100g (4oz) dried pitted prunes
50g (2oz) sugar
275ml (½ pint) fruit juice
275ml (½ pint) water
10-12 slices bread

Peel and break up the satsumas. Chop the dried fruit. Put the sugar, water, fruit juice and dried fruit into a saucepan. Simmer for 20 minutes. Add the satsumas and simmer for five more minutes. Use the mixture in the same way as the fruit in summer pudding.

Fit a small plate over the pudding. Put weights such as tins on top. Leave it to chill overnight in a refrigerator.

Take the plate and weight off the pudding. Put a large plate over it. Turn the plate and basin upside down.

Shake the basin and lift it off slowly, leaving the pudding on the plate. Pour the cup of fruit over it.

Pasta dishes

Pasta, like potatoes or rice, is a basic food. This means that you can use it in all sorts of different meals and add lots of tasty things to it. There are many kinds of pasta. This recipe uses spaghetti but you could try using other pasta shapes, like shells or twists.

Spaghetti bolognese

You will need:
1 onion
1 green pepper
100g (4oz) mushrooms
1 tbs cooking oil
250g (8oz) minced beef
400g (14oz) tin tomatoes
1 tsp mixed herbs
1 rounded tbs tomato purée
salt
250g (8oz) spaghetti
some grated cheese

kitchen knife, chopping board, two large saucepans, wooden spoon, tin opener, fork, colander, grater, plate

Chop the onion, pepper and mushrooms. Put the oil into a saucepan. Turn a ring or burner to medium heat.

Heat the oil. Add the onion, mushrooms and pepper and cook gently for four minutes until soft.

Add the minced beef. Stir it until it is all brown and there are no red bits left. This is called browning.

Open the tin of tomatoes. Stir into the mixture with the tomato purée, mixed herbs and a pinch of salt.

Serve the spaghetti bolognese straight away with grated cheese.

Vegetarian sauce

Make a vegetarian sauce by leaving out the minced beef. You could add more mushrooms, another green pepper, a red pepper or some black olives instead.

For a link to a website where you can explore many different pasta shapes, go to www.usborne-quicklinks.com

If the sauce begins to spit, turn the heat down further.

Bring to the **boil**, then turn the heat down low. **Simmer** for 30 minutes, stirring from time to time.

Cook the spaghetti in the other saucepan (see below). Drain, then serve onto plates. Spoon the sauce on top.

The pasta test

If you cook pasta for too long it goes slimy and sticks together, so you need to test it as it cooks. Take some out with a fork. Let it cool, then taste it. It is cooked when just firm, not too soft but not crunchy.

Cooking pasta

Half-fill a large saucepan with water. Add a pinch of salt. Turn on a burner or ring. Bring to the boil.

Place the pasta carefully in the water. If it is spaghetti, push it down gradually with a spoon as it softens.

Stir and bring to the boil again. Turn the heat down. Simmer for the time it says on the packet and test it.

Add 1 tbs oil to the pan to stop it from sticking.

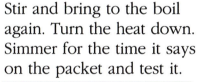

Most pasta cooks in about ten minutes.

When cooked, ask an adult to help you drain the pasta by tipping it into a colander over the sink.

Cooking with eggs

Eggs can be cooked in lots of different ways. One of the special ways you can use them is to cook things that are very light to eat. You do this by whisking the egg white before you use it. This adds lots of air to it and makes it go white and frothy.

Lemon surprise pudding

You will need:

1 large lemon	25g (1oz) butter
2 eggs	150ml (¼ pint) milk
100g (4oz) sugar	50g (2oz) self-raising flour

grater, small plate, kitchen knife, chopping board, lemon squeezer, mixing bowl, saucer, egg cup, cup, small bowl, sieve, wooden spoon, whisk, metal spoon, medium oven-proof dish, oven gloves

Separating eggs

Crack the egg on the side of a cup. Break it open over a small saucer, being careful not to break the yolk.

Put an egg cup over the egg yolk. Tip the white into a small bowl. Lift off the egg cup and tip the yolk into a cup.

GET HELP

Try not to grate the white pith underneath the rind.

Turn the oven to 190°C (375°F, Gas Mark 5). **Grate** the rind from the lemon, using the fine holes.

Separate the eggs (see left). Put the egg white into a small bowl and put the yolks into the mixing bowl.

Cut the lemon in half and squeeze the juice from it. Put the juice into the mixing bowl with the rind.

The mixture is quite runny.

Sieve the flour into the mixing bowl. Add the sugar and butter. **Beat** together well, then beat in the milk.

This dish is called a "surprise" because when you cut through the spongy top you find a lovely lemony sauce at the bottom.

Whisking egg whites

Recipes often ask you to whisk egg white until stiff. This means that when you lift the whisk it stands up in little triangles or peaks.

With a hand whisk, turn your wrist round and round quickly. It can take quite a long time for the white to go stiff.

To use a rotary whisk, hold it up straight and turn the handle. Ask an adult to help with an electric whisk.

Whisk the egg white until stiff (see right). **Fold** into the mixture. Pour the mixture into the oven-proof dish.

HOT
Use the middle shelf.

TURN IT OFF

Cook it for 35 minutes. If it is firm and golden brown, it is ready. If not, cook it for five more minutes.

Folding in - p.11

Cooking with rice

You can use rice as a main part of many different meals. For example, you could cook savoury rice and eat it on its own, or boil some rice and cook something else to eat with it. Try it with chicken parcels (see pages 12-13).

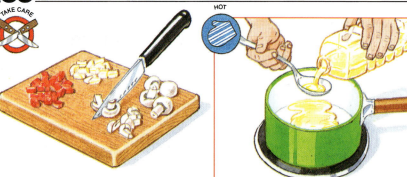

🍅 Savoury rice

You will need:
100g (4oz) mushrooms
1 red pepper
1 onion
400g (14oz) tin tomatoes
2 tbs cooking oil
250g (8oz) long grain white rice
100g (4oz) peas or green beans
275ml (½ pint) hot water
1 tbs soy sauce
pinch of salt
1 vegetable stock cube

kitchen knife
chopping board
tin opener
tablespoon
large saucepan
wooden spoon
measuring jug

Wash the mushrooms and **chop** them into quarters. Chop the pepper and onion. Open the tin of tomatoes.

Turn on a ring or burner to low heat and put the oil in a saucepan. Heat it very gently for a minute or two.

You could try eating your savoury rice with chopsticks.

*For a link to a website where you can find out more about rice and learn how to make Japanese rice balls, go to **www.usborne-quicklinks.com***

Add the onion. Stir and cook for four minutes. Add the mushrooms and red pepper. Cook for three more minutes.

Add the rice. Cook for two minutes, stirring all the time with a wooden spoon to stop it from sticking.

Boiling rice

1. Weigh out 50g (2oz) rice for each person. Half-fill a big saucepan with water and add a pinch of salt. Turn on a ring or burner.

2. Bring the water to the **boil.** Add the rice. Bring to the boil again, then simmer the rice for the time it says on the packet.

Most rice cooks in about 20-25 minutes.

3. After the right amount of time, take out a few grains of rice with a fork to test them. They should be firm, but not crunchy.

Let it cool slightly before you taste it.

4. When the rice is cooked, ask an adult to help you tip it into a sieve over the sink. Shake all the water out of the sieve.

Add the tin of tomatoes, peas or beans, water, soy sauce and salt. Crumble the stock cube into the mixture.

Mix everything together. **Simmer** for 15-20 minutes, stirring gently from time to time to stop it from sticking.

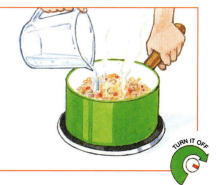

Test the rice (see above). If it is not yet cooked and the rice is getting dry, add a little more water.

Find out more: Chopping - p.13   Boiling and simmering - p.14

21

Rubbing in and rolling out

Rubbing in is a skill you sometimes use to mix butter or margarine into flour. You often have to rub in when you make dough mixtures like pastry dough or scone dough. You can roll out most kinds of dough with a rolling pin.

Apple scones

You will need:
1 medium cooking apple
250g (8oz) self-raising flour
1 level tsp baking powder
75g (3oz) margarine
50g (2oz) sugar
50ml (2fl oz) milk
a little extra milk

baking tray, kitchen roll, chopping board, vegetable peeler, kitchen knife, mixing bowl, sieve, rounded knife, wooden spoon, rolling pin, fish slice, pastry brush, oven gloves, wire rack

Rubbing in

1. To rub in, cut the margarine or butter into pieces. Add it to the flour.

2. Mix and cut with a rounded knife until the butter is coated in flour.

3. Rub the mixture between your fingers, lifting it and letting it drop.

4. When the butter is mixed in well, the mixture looks like breadcrumbs.

Turn the oven to 200°C (400°F, Gas Mark 6). **Grease** the baking tray with some margarine.

Hold the apple firmly. Peel it with a vegetable peeler by scraping towards you with the sharp edge.

Hold the apple, making a bridge with your fingers. Cut it in half, then into quarters.

Use a small kitchen knife.

Hold each quarter firmly. Carefully cut the core from each one, then chop them all into little pieces.

Sieve the flour and baking powder into a mixing bowl. Rub in the margarine. Stir in the sugar.

Rolling out

Sprinkle flour over a clean, dry surface. Put the dough onto it. Rub flour over the rolling pin.

Add the apple. Stir in the milk and make a ball of dough. It should be soft but not sticky.

Roll out the ball of dough (see right) until it is a round shape about 2½cm (1in) thick.

Apple scones are good as part of a picnic or packed lunch.

Cut the dough into eight pieces. Place them on the baking tray with a fish slice. Brush with milk.

Press the dough down a little then roll gently and evenly. If the rolling pin sticks, add more flour.

To make a round shape, roll a little, then stop. Turn the dough slightly and shape the edge. Roll again.

Bake for 20-25 minutes on the top shelf. They are ready when golden brown. Cool on a wire rack.

Find out more: Greasing tins - p.10

Making bread

When you make bread you use yeast, which makes the bread dough rise and the bread light to eat. The yeast also makes the dough become smooth and springy. This means that it is easy to make it into different shapes before you cook it. There are three shapes suggested here, but you could try making other ones.

Bread rolls

For 8 rolls you will need :
150ml (¼ pint) warm water
1 level tsp dried yeast
1 level tsp sugar
250g (8oz) strong plain
  white flour (not
  self-raising flour)
½ level tsp salt
a little milk

tablespoon, small bowl, teaspoon, sieve, mixing bowl, wooden spoon, plastic foodwrap, baking tray, kitchen roll, kitchen knife, pastry brush, oven gloves

Here you can see what cottage rolls and twists look like when they are cooked.

The water must be just warm, not hot.

Put 2 tbs of the warm water into a small bowl. Add the yeast and sugar and stir everything together well.

Leave the mixture for about 15 minutes.

Leave the bowl in a warm place, such as an airing cupboard, until the mixture becomes frothy on top.

Sieve the flour and salt into a mixing bowl. Make a hole in the middle. Pour in the frothy yeast mixture.

Add the rest of the warm water. Mix with a wooden spoon until it all sticks together to make a dough.

For a link to a website where you can do an experiment to find out how yeast makes bread rise, go to **www.usborne-quicklinks.com**

The dough will become about twice as big as it was before.

Make the dough into a ball with your hands. Knead it for ten minutes (see below). Put it back into the bowl.

Cover the bowl with plastic foodwrap and put it in a warm place. Leave it to rise for at least an hour.

Turn the oven to 220°C (425°F, Gas Mark 7). **Grease** a baking tray. Knead the dough again for five minutes.

Put a little ball on top of a bigger one to make a cottage roll.

To make a twist, make a sausage then tie it in a knot.

Bake for five more minutes if not cooked.

Cut the dough into eight pieces. Make them into balls, or shape them into cottage rolls or twists, as above.

Put the rolls back in a warm place for 15 minutes to let them rise again, then brush them with a little milk.

Bake the rolls for about 15 minutes. They are cooked if they sound hollow when you tap them underneath.

Kneading

Sprinkle flour over a clean, dry surface. Stretch the dough out, pushing away from you.

Fold the dough over, then push it back into a ball. Stretch it out again. Keep stretching and folding it.

Stop when the dough is stretchy and you can make a ball that is round and smooth.

You often have to knead for about ten minutes.

Find out more: Greasing tins - p.10

A pizza meal

You can use bread dough to make the base for pizzas. This recipe gives some ideas for toppings, but you could try all kinds of tasty things like fresh tomato, onion, black olives or different kinds of pepper. Some of these toppings are on the pizza in the photograph. You could make a green salad to eat with your pizza.

Mini pizzas

For four pizzas you will need:

250g (8oz) bread dough (see pages 24-25)
4 rounded tbs tomato purée
4 tbs water
100g (4oz) cheese
50g (2oz) mushrooms
1 large slice cooked ham
1 green pepper

utensils for making dough (see page 24), chopping board, kitchen knife, small bowl, tablespoon, grater, plate, two baking trays, kitchen roll, wooden spoon, colander, bowl for salad

For a green salad you will need:

a small lettuce
cucumber
two celery sticks

colander, large bowl, kitchen knife, chopping board

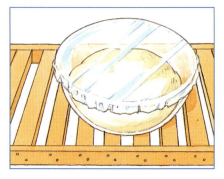

Follow the recipe for bread on pages 24-25, as far as leaving the dough for an hour in a warm place.

While the dough is rising, **slice** the ham, pepper and mushrooms. Mix the tomato purée and water in a bowl.

Find out more: Slicing - p.7, p.13

For a link to a website where you can try out another pizza recipe, and many other tasty snacks, go to www.usborne-quicklinks.com

Grate the cheese onto a plate. **Grease** two baking trays and turn the oven to 220°C (425°F, Gas Mark 7).

When the dough has risen, **knead** it for five minutes. Cut it into four equal pieces and shape them into balls.

Making a green salad

To prepare a lettuce, take off any broken leaves. Break off the rest of the leaves. Wash them in a colander.

Use cold water to wash the lettuce.

Don't worry if they are not quite round.

Put two balls of dough onto each baking tray. Push and stretch them into round, flat shapes with your hands.

Spread the tomato mixture over the pizzas with a wooden spoon. Don't spread it right to the edges.

Hold the leaves down and shake them dry. Put them into a large bowl and shred them with your fingers.

Chop the cucumber into little pieces. Wash the celery sticks. Chop off the ends, then slice them into little pieces.

Arrange the toppings evenly over the tomato mixture, then sprinkle the grated cheese on top.

They are ready when the edges are brown and crisp.

Cook for 20 minutes. Give one tray ten minutes on the top shelf, then swap it with the one on the middle shelf.

Add to the lettuce and mix.

Grating - p.6   Greasing tins - p.10   Kneading - p.25   Chopping - p.7

More about baking

To make some kinds of cake or biscuit, such as flapjacks, you melt some of the ingredients together in a saucepan before putting them into the oven. This is called the 'melting method' of baking. When you have made them you can decorate them with all sorts of things. Here you can see some ideas for decorations, but you could try using other ones.

Flapjacks

You will need:
150g (6oz) margarine
3 tbs golden syrup
75g (3oz) brown sugar
200g (8oz) rolled oats

18cm x 28cm (7in x 11in) baking tray, kitchen paper, medium-sized saucepan, wooden spoon, oven gloves, rounded knife, wire rack

For decorating the flapjacks you will need:
100g (4oz) plain or milk chocolate
decorations such as glacé cherries or sweets

small heat-proof bowl, small saucepan, wooden spoon, oven gloves, teaspoon

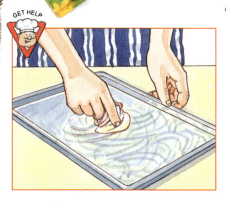

GET HELP

Turn the oven on to 180°C, (350°F, Gas Mark 4). **Grease** the baking tray with some margarine on kitchen paper.

HOT

Turn on a ring or burner to low heat. Put the sugar, syrup and margarine into the larger saucepan.

Melting chocolate

Break the chocolate into pieces. Put it into a small bowl. Turn on a ring or burner to low heat.

Half-fill a small saucepan with water and stand the bowl in it. Heat the water, but don't let it boil.

When the chocolate has melted, lift the bowl out carefully. Use straight away (see below).

Stir with a wooden spoon.

Wear oven gloves.

Melt the mixture gently, stirring with a wooden spoon. When melted, take the pan off the heat.

Stir in the oats. Tip the mixture into the baking tray. Flatten it over with the back of a wooden spoon.

Decorating cakes and biscuits

Scoop up some melted chocolate with a teaspoon. Let it drip over the cakes. Melt the chocolate again if it begins to go hard.

Make patterns, or smooth the chocolate over with the spoon.

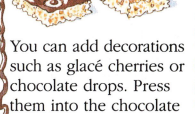

You can add decorations such as glacé cherries or chocolate drops. Press them into the chocolate while it is still soft.

You could decorate brownies (see pages 10-11).

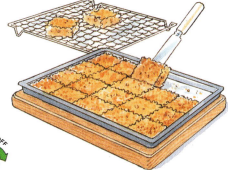

Bake on the middle shelf of the oven for 20-25 minutes. The flapjacks should be golden brown when cooked.

Cut into squares with a rounded knife. Allow to cool for 10-15 minutes, then take them out of the tin.

29

Making sauces

You can make delicious dishes out of simple things like pasta by adding a sauce to them. There are many different kinds of sauce. Here you can find out how to make white sauce, which is made with milk, flour and butter. In this recipe you then add cheese to make it into a cheese sauce, which is really tasty.

Tuna bake

You will need:
150g (6oz) cheese
200g (7oz) tin tuna
200g (7oz) tin
  sweetcorn
250g (8oz) pasta
  (macaroni or any
  other pasta shape)
salt
a tomato and
  some fresh
  parsley

To make white sauce you will need:
50g (2oz) margarine
  or butter
50g (2oz) plain flour
500ml (1 pint) milk

grater, plate, tin opener, big saucepan, colander, medium saucepan, wooden spoon, measuring jug, whisk, oven-proof dish, oven gloves, kitchen knife, chopping board

To decorate the bake, arrange slices of tomato and little bits of parsley on top before serving.

Grate the cheese. Open the tins of sweetcorn and tuna and drain them into the sink.

Cook the pasta in a big saucepan for ten minutes. When cooked, drain with a sieve or a colander.

Make a white sauce in a medium saucepan (see right). When it thickens, take it off the heat.

For a link to a website where you can find lots more fun and simple recipes to try at home, go to www.usborne-quicklinks.com

Stir 100g (4oz) of the cheese into the sauce. Add the tuna, sweetcorn and a pinch of salt.

Stir the mixture well, then pour it all into the big saucepan with the pasta. Mix everything together.

Making white sauce

Turn a burner or ring to medium heat. Melt the margarine gently.

Add the flour. Stir for one minute with a wooden spoon. Take off the heat.

Add a little of the milk. Stir well, then add a little more and mix it in.

Keep stirring in the milk a little at a time until it is all mixed in.

It will be a runny mixture.

Put the saucepan back on the heat. Heat up the sauce, stirring all the time.

As it heats up, the sauce will thicken. **Simmer** and stir for one minute.

Beat out any lumps with a whisk.

Spoon the mixture into an oven-proof dish. Scatter the rest of the cheese over the top.

Take the grill pan from under the grill to make more space. Turn the grill on to full heat.

Put the dish under the grill for about ten minutes, or until the cheese is golden brown and bubbling.

Cheesy pasta

Follow the steps for tuna bake, but use 250g (8oz) cheese. Leave out the tuna. Leave in the sweetcorn if you want to.

Cooking skills

This page explains some of the cooking skills and words that appear in this book and tells you a little bit more about them.

Beating - mixing something quickly and firmly with a wooden spoon or electric mixer.

Boiling - when a liquid or runny mixture is heated so that it becomes very hot and bubbles a lot.

Browning - cooking red meat, like beef, in hot oil until it turns brown all over.

Chopping - cutting something into chunks with a kitchen knife.

Cracking an egg - tapping the egg sharply on the edge of a cup or small bowl, putting your thumbs into the gap you have made and pulling the eggshell apart.

Creaming - beating margarine or butter and sugar together so that they become light and creamy.

Folding in - mixing one ingredient into another very gently with a metal spoon or rounded knife.

Grating - scraping a piece of food down the holes on a grater to make it into small pieces.

Kneading - pulling, pushing and folding dough so that it becomes smooth and stretchy.

Peeling - taking off the skin of a vegetable or fruit by cutting into it with a vegetable peeler, then scraping towards you.

Rolling out - making dough or pastry into a flat shape with a rolling pin.

Rubbing in - mixing flour and butter or margarine together with a knife, then your fingertips, to make a crumbly mixture.

Sieving - getting rid of any lumps in something like flour by putting it into a sieve and shaking it over a bowl. You can also push it through the sieve with the back of a metal spoon.

Simmering - when a liquid or runny mixture is hot, but only bubbling a little bit.

Slicing - cutting something with a kitchen knife to make thin pieces.

Squeezing a lemon - getting the juice from a lemon by putting one half over the top of a lemon squeezer and twisting it to the left and to the right.

Whisking - adding lots of air to something by turning it quickly with a hand whisk, rotary whisk or electric whisk.

First published in 1995 by Usborne Publishing Ltd, 83–85 Saffron Hill, London EC1N 8RT, England. www.usborne.com
Copyright © 2003, 1995 Usborne Publishing Ltd. First published in America in 1996. This edition published in America in 2004. The name Usborne and the devices ♀ ⊕ are Trade Marks of Usborne Publishing Ltd. All rights reserved. No part of this publication may be reproduced, stored in a retrieval system, or transmitted in any form or by any means, electronic, mechanical, photocopying, recording or otherwise, without the prior permission of the publisher. Printed in Belgium.
Usborne Publishing is not responsible, and does not accept liability, for the availability or content of any website other than its own, or for any exposure to harmful, offensive, or inaccurate material which may appear on the Web. Usborne Publishing will have no liability for any damage or loss caused by viruses that may be downloaded as a result of browsing the sites we recommend.